THE ARCANE AURORA

PEARL

ISBN 979-888606995-2

To:

Mom & Dad, who gave me the wings;

Angel, who flew with me.

Contents

Contents

Contents

"With hearts, so not drenched in fears, pour open to the wide horizons, the infinities of your innards…

And in the process you are reborn. For you did first to live a story of your existence and now, born again, to tell stories which ought to be told for those to behold."

~Pearl

Acknowledgements

My gratitude extends primarily to my family. Mom and Dad, who gave me a spark in every field accessible and the freedom of choice to cherish the one most loved. Had it not been for the artistic freedom and the discipline, this book would've been a thought.

I thank, with all my heart, the first reader of the book, my eternal dose of encouragement to publish it, the feedback house, my little sister: Angel; for all the moments I bought from her to pen down a couplet, for going out of her way to read my poetry and for every single time she called me her "Favourite author", Thank You!

I express my deepest thanks to my literary mentors, Ms. Monika and Mr. Puneet, for not just teaching me to hold the pen and write but to hold the pen and create.

I am indebted to Dr. Solomon David for being my beacon through the spiritual journey and edifying my soul with his profound outlook.

I must also thank the Notion press Team for being responsive and assistive around the clock for every little query throughout the process.

Finally, I'd like to thank the myriads of indispensible people Mr. Harcharan, Ms. Nidhi Pandey, Ms. Shalini, Ms. Mona and others, who had a pivotal part in bringing this dream to fruition.

Dear Reader,

With all my heart, I thank you for picking this poetic fable as your next read. I have put in earnest efforts, to make your journey from here on, in these pages, comfortable and engaging.

'Poetry is spontaneous overflow of powerful feelings: it takes its origin from emotions recollected in tranquility' says Wordsworth. But I sincerely admit, spontaneity didn't present itself to me until the last two years. I started as, what I'd like to call, a "People's poet"; writing poems for people I revered.

Eventually, kindled by the works of Wordsworth, Frost, Keats, Tennyson, Tagore, Whitman and many more, I entered this magnificent world of fantasies and more. Soon, spontaneity possessed me and I would find myself scribbling in free time. This led to my first chapbook, 'Poetry Given Life' being published in July 2019. During the COVID-19 era, I got a chance to relish and absorb literature in its purest form under the guidance of Ms. Monika.

On a tranquil afternoon of 2021, as I was rereading my past works, I stumbled upon my aforementioned book. I was an amateur then, I admit. After a few moments, I found my hands typing on Google, "Can you republish a book?" And the answer was YES! Thus, I collected all my poems, long or short, rhymed or not rhymed, to form this collection. After a little editing here and a little rhyming there, I, hereby, entrust to you, the book farer, my treasured soul, which I have in nights so deep, poured open to ink

and which these august pages have held ever too lovingly.
Happy Reading!

Your Humble Author

February 2022

"When the first of steps shall be taken,

In the blanket of the morn,

A journey of thousand miles shall begin,

A new "YOU" shall be born;

For every journey, short or long,

Begins at the ardent Dawn."

1. The Brown-eyed Man

In the freshly mown grass I walked,
Away into the woods, under the azure skies,
Towards me flew a tanned hawk,
With extremely familiar nut-brown eyes,

Lost in thoughts I was transported,
A man stood beside me,
We walked towards the orchids,
He looked towards me with glee.

Another memory, another day,
The man was sitting with a miserable face,
I asked him, and he didn't tell me anyway,
It felt as if he'd lost a terrible race.

He toiled and struggled and sacrificed,
I asked, "For whom you do all this?"
"For you," he silently cried.
The reply left me enriched in bliss.

The next day came with an expeditious speed,
"I want the toys and the books," I cried.

He bought me one and pacified my greed,
His solemn words made him my guide.

My eyes were swollen and drenched in tears,
"What is it?" he asked, calmly with a hopeful smile,
With one gasp, I burst out with all my ugly fears,
And he soothed me and hugged me for a while.

Back to the lovely woods I came,
Thinking where I had been lost,
A man walked near, he was the same,
In the sun, his half-bald head glossed.

I stared into those deep-brown eyes,
Ran and hugged him with all my might,
He embraced me with a lovely delight,
"Thank You Pa! Love You!" I fondly cried.

2. O Sky, My Sky

In a little click as the hand beheld
I held it out too more,
For someone loving a lovely shore
Would take it ever more
Who that wondrous soul is?
I wonder day by day.
I cry out to the world without,
What is it meant to say?

Hold someone, this happy hand,
Don't leave it out amiss,
For I am a maiden happy said,
A little child to be gladly met.

Yonder skies that stand above,
They hear the fingers snapping
And looking and watching they say,
'O little lovely beauty of day
I hold your hand deeply today.
Don't wait for someone to hold it too.
Two hands you have:
One for me and one for you!'

I hold the skies,
For my dreams lie
To fly to eternity, I ever cry.

O sky, my love, hold me true
For if this hand be blessed,
So am I for you!
I hold my hand strongly too,
But one stays now,
In your blossomed hue!

I love ye sky
Nor human anigh;
For human will hold
For days too short,
And after life is lost,
He'll climb your mast.

O sky, my sky! I call again,
Nothing in my love, do I feign;
If in the end, I be yours
Then why not today,
Should I climb your doors?

For if any human be I earthly love,
We'll fly up to you in a moment's shrug.

So love my human and love you too
For you'll unite us
After the deadly blues
And thus, we'll stay,
With you too.

O give ye shelter, ye lovely hue!
For, my sky, after we lose
You'll begin the story all anew!
You'll keep the love alive,
For after our form does die,
The tale will be told
In my lovely skies.

3. Shadows and Lights

Two spots pointed
In the illumination of the sun.
Hide they: the sun behind them,
And get enlightened in its shadow.

A bond that leaves behind,
And hides the illumination,
In the search of darkness,
To the brightness of their souls.

Let us hide all the bright sides,
And cherish the dark ones,
For they need a chance to be chosen
And explored, for the mysteries they hold.

In the shadow of ourselves under the brightness,
Let's explore once more,
What lies and what does not,
For it is the shadow that makes us different.

Out of our shadows,
Let's examine the unknown

And name the mystic nameless.
For it is the shadow that says a lot more,
Than we, ourselves, do.
We are always different in our shadows,
Than we in goodness of truths are.

4. The Longest Slumber

By the blasphemous whim of an outrageous slumber,
He rose as from dead to life again,
Embraced his loving wife in his duly lovable arms,
And then laid down again as dead,
To never wake again.
It was a whim,
Of that same outrageous slumber,
That made it seem like living;
But for soul that
To death been lost,
Had gone beyond the realms of Earth
And entered the heavens above,
She cried not a tear of guilt;
Just embraced him in her arms,
And kissed him once more,
For if lost in life they were,
In love they lived forever-more!

5. The Flute Seller

And there he came with wooden sticks,
And some carefully chosen metal picks;
Flute seller, was he professionally called,
"Bhaiya!" "Uncle" the world bawled.

He played himself the instrument of wind,
That man somewhat tall and dark skinned.
He walked and walked spreading melodies around,
Till in his sound the whole town was drowned.

The frivolous wandering children
Who basked in the glistening sun,
Ran all out at once to their parents,
To bother them with their monetary laments.

From our heighted windows we saw:
The producer of such music, without a flaw,
This too curious a seldom-seen sight
And thus the impending emotional delights!

He played and played and little thought,
And soon, those sticks were happily bought;

From street to street, I watched him go,
There standing above at my window.

The flutes now so freshly bought,
I could, in every little hand spot,
They played their songs, bland and confused,
Like, with chocolates, pickles were fused;
"Ew! That would taste gross," you'd say.
That's the true point I mean to convey:
The harmony of our musician curbed,
By these young roamers perturbed.

Yet he resumed after the short term sales,
Those soothing tiny musical tales,
The birds' chirrup added to the sonic pleasure,
In those lazy afternoon hours of leisure.

The notes drove near and my head peeped out,
"I'll buy one!" the heart wanted to shout
But the fear of asking for too needless a thing,
Made my melophilic heart deeply sting;

And under silent torment I wanted him to stay,
But there with swift steps, he walked away,
To streets beyond, he went to trade,
And slowly, I heard the dulcet tunes fade.

Just that one stick from that stacked galore,
Had I even bought to just merely adore,
Would have bought me joys and more,
Traditions and stories of the Indian folklore.

But there I bid him adieu,
To rest in life's warm hue,
He won my heart and made my day,
"Thank You!" is all I could then say!

6. Thrifty Knaves

The very little heart that I had to give,
I gave it out to the world to hold.
But those thrifty knaves of world without,
Tore it bit by bit,
Till all remained were shattered pieces,
Broken by treason and deceit.
It has been glued together to hold
And now pieces do recover;
But as I look back at times
It has been long ago,
Yet every little crack speaks of a tale,
Too haunting for my otherwise cheery soul.

7. Just a Moment

Well, sometimes it's just a moment
Just a blink of the eye at the brink of the ocean,
Or just a tick of a clock chiming at twelve
Or just a cycle of electron around its proton
Or just a transmission of neural signal
Or just passage of a beam of light
Or Just a single vibration of the molecules
Or just a beat of the heart pumping blood
Or just a click of beak of the parrot outside
Or just a gust of wind across your body
Or just a cracking of a dropped glass;
Well, sometimes it really is a moment that could've changed it
all.

8. Just a Dream

The more the flies buzzed,
The more the drowsiness flared,
Inside the depth of my fathomless eyes;
Profound slumber overtook me,
And I drowned deeper and deeper,
Into the obfuscation of reality.
There I was, standing amidst the crowd,
Waving and cheering, clapping and swaying,
Bliss filling up my veins,
The cheers grew louder,
And all of a sudden,
My head lay there,
Miles from my body,
I panted and realized,
'It was just a dream.'

9. The Missed Meows

The while he was here,
I hit him with the broom;
But now, when he's gone,
I stay dipped in gloom.
O why nature's wish is so!
Once love is lost,
It leaves you so low.

His meows were noises then,
Which I yearn now to hear.
How neglected did I leave him,
When he was, in life, near.

The day he was born,
To the day I saw him go,
I never felt forlorn.
But all that stays now,
Is relentless woe.
'Simba' was he named,
That little child of cat.
"SIMBA!!" Came the beating,
When he brought home a rat.

I miss the long cuddles
And him bathing in puddles;
The heavenly touch of his fur,
And the thus following purr.

His round rusks from the bakery,
Mixed with warm milk,
Made his meal for the day,
And left him in great bliss.

All he did was sleep all day,
"Lazy Simba!" I'd often say;
I'd capture his photographs,
While he happily slept,
I'd disturb his sleep always,
And keep him unkempt.

He was free to roam about:
The one thing I made sure of.
But who knew freedom was so costly,
And the price would be his life?

The dog of the street and my Simba,
Broke into a fight,
To declare who is more might;
I wasn't there to see:

My brave one perish away.
Yet from people who saw,
I know he stood upright.
The battle was lost,
And so was the fighter,
But I am sure it was well fought,
For I know the feeble body I loved,
Which loved to look for risks,
If one thing he taught me,
Is life is brighter with risks.

He saw not the sunrise,
And I saw not him.
Life was lost to him,
And my love was lost to me.

10. Some Gray Hearts

I gazed and gazed into the vastness,
Did nothing but gazed with wonder,
Could not have been baffled less,
When the sky roared in a fierce thunder.

What was it then, I couldn't say,
But in my chair I hopelessly lay,
And stroking my chin, deliberately thought,
What to me the day had brought.

Fresh air didn't surprise in the morn,
For I met with burning trees forlorn,
Such an abomination was dearly bought,
For we had caused nature to rot.

The scorching heat took my friend away,
And I was left in shock to stay;
There was only one thing to exclaim,
"My dear fellow humans to blame!"

"Oh! Alas! Not again, this miserable power outage."
How am I in my activities supposed to engage?

With power being cut 10 times a day,
Who in this troublesome case should I blame?

The storm is, of course, known to have done it,
But I don't believe it as all the other misfits,
It's the fruit of our doing we reap,
And let me assure you the bruise is deep.

Had we been prudent, had we not slain
Our darling brethren for our gain,
They would've lived to bring some rain,
And helped us out in order to sustain.

But we are vulnerable to folly and it isn't a sin
Unless we are obstinate with a haughty grin,
But my crying is useless, my cribbing just a waste,
For we are too much engaged to make any haste.

"You say it always but it's most futile;
You wish fruitlessly for us and nature to reconcile.
But have you had the courage to say?
What have you done for it till this day?"

Let me answer this by asking you:
Did you ever observe nature's hue?
Did you ever cherish what it had to proffer?
Or were you too busy a scoffer?

Let me assure you I was not,
For what has to be done is not lot,
Just leave her blemished under the inflictions of our race,
But make sure no more of our iniquity she has to embrace.

You'll be amazed the magic of her hands,
The scars will disappear off her lands,
For this is the magic of most splendid charm,
Expressed when we'd leave her unharmed.

Another thunder revived me up;
My infliction on her I did lockup,
And now relishing her with utmost mesmerism,
I was seeing her hues through a filtered vision.

The day was gray, the ceiling low,
I didn't know which thoughts to sow,
I was gloomy to think of her pain,
Yet I knew thinking of it was vain.

I knew I boasted of my love of her,
Yet I accepted it as it were,
For to be absolute would be a sin,
And in that case there would be no win.

After all I say at length, I must admit:

That sometimes I do fall a victim,
To the enjoyment of some petty delights,
Which might be capable of giving nature frights.

Yet, the hope lies in trying as best as I can,
That may be capable of extending her span,
For of all things, it's never too old to say,
That human hearts are ultimately grey!

11. If Only I Had

Patience in my aspect,
Tranquility in my air,
I stepped down the aisle
On a heap of roses red,
To my unhappy death bed.
It wasn't with thorns adorned,
Yet no one to cry or mourn;
Advancing towards my earthly brim,
'The journey was over,' I heard me think.

But what was the crime
That I ought to lay,
On this bed, on a ghostly day?
Yet the heart was warm
With the love so sore
For whom I entered death's door.

They would live
And on their lips,
Would stay my name
In a blissful hiss.
For I who die for them,

For a perjury I committed not;
This is the least I do in love,
For those who did it for me,
Through life's moments so more.

I don't cry for nothing at all;
The only sin that ever was,
Is not hug them all at once,
For when life was a kinder hue,
I had a messed up view.
But the blurred vision now
Stands upright,
And through my better sight,
I should've thanked them once in a while;

But now, as life ebbs away,
In regret I sway;
If not in life I stayed with them,
I hope in death I'll be a part of them.

12. The Limit Is The Sky

A day of beauty, a day of joys,
Not too much money, not too many strives,
Seated in the middle,
Looked up at the sky,
Sang my heart out,
And bid a hearty good-bye,
To all those things that kept me back,
Letting go of the past,
Just you fly and fly,
'Cause when you're determined:
The limit is the sky.

13. Changes

When the days are cold
And the nights don't hold
I will make me a gift
Send it far at some width
Climb on it some big day
Just to make my way
Through the clouds and the skies
Through the truths and the lies
Dive in the oceans deep within
Cry out for life in a swing,
Make my heart go mad
Never be low or a little sad
Unleash the power in me
Fly to the stars with it
Never look back at the ground
They are where I belong
Unleash the beast in me
I have the power to see
Beyond the blinding mist
Let's give my life a twist
Create a dazzling life
Above the cries and the strives

THE ARCANE AURORA

Be happily unique always
Carve your own pathways
Things would change
May get out of range
But as long you stand strong
Your whole life will throng!

14. Death

And here I come,
Into your welcoming arms,
Embrace me,
Cuddle me,
Keep me warm,
I am an illusion,
Just take a deep breath,
My dear friend,
They call me Death.

15. The Trip

The weather reflected in the crystal sky,
I was wonderstruck, couldn't say why?
And there came gently pouring rain,
Incapable of even wetting the lane,

The flowers were dreamily lovely,
Those lilies, lotuses all gladly blooming;
The steep turns were no less than a nightmare.
The monkey's maze, the horror house,
The boating race, the climbing mouse,
All were worthy of an applause;
Not for a second in this dreamland,
Could we ever pause.

After days which come long after,
Something still made me stir;
The memories reflected in the crystal sky,
I was mesmerized, couldn't say why?

16. Happy Birthday!

'Ding dong bell.'
Hey, who the hell?
'Your friend from class 7,
Now proceeding to class 11.'
Oh yeah, but why did you ring the bell?
'There's something I want to tell.'
What is it? I want to know.
'Catch the words that I throw:'
Don't play around tell me NOW!
'First form an unbreakable vow.'
I'm not staying here for your games.
'Hey, don't leave, hear my claims!'
No, thanks. I'd better leave.
'Don't leave it on my sleeve!'
Okay. I give you a full minute to bawl.
'"HAPPY BIRTHDAY" is the sum of it all.'
Is that all? You're a fool with no head.
'Well that's something well-said.'
And yeah, thank you for your wish.
'I pray for your health and bliss,'
Go no more, that's enough.
'May you always smile and laugh,

And achieve successes beyond your mind,
And all the hearty pleasures you bind.'

17. Demons

If words call you dark and deep,
And to the dreadful ocean
You find you seep:
Cry loud, the darkness out
Call it a day, and then you shout,
And shut the demons out the door.

If they still haunt you ever more
By their name you call them so,
For name is fear and fear in the name
Catches you in the middle of the lane,
Cry and shout for help again.

The pain is real; they'll come for help:
The demons will go to devil's hell,
And thus, ringing your fancy's knell,
Pull you out of the darkened well.
You were lost and found again
By that one soul of love;
Love, true love and no game;
'I am here' you'll hear them say,
And just when solitude ate you away,

You'll see them boldly save the day!

It's just a faction of the vagrant mind,
Which haunts you at various times.
The heart seems to fade away,
In loneliness you find you sway,
Shadows befriend, and light befoes
And all that's left is doleful woes.

But hear the tale from a different soul,
That you love and are loved by;
Calm down your heaving sighs,
Hug them once, love them twice,
Fill your day with their smiles,
Let them know of the demons,
And let them slay it for you.

They won't resist or rebuke you more
Only in light will they see you glow;
And in times that pass as blink of eye,
The battle will be won with a hearty smile!

Yes, they'll stay and play with you,
They never left your life's view.
Told you, the nomadic mind was it,
Making you a gloomy misfit;
And now you rejoice in their wake,

O your friends, those not fake!

18. Life

The most beautiful gift
That gives our happiness a lift.

Every wonder enriched in it.
Every dream is filled in it.

Sometimes we forget its worth
As we fill it with too much mirth.

Several moments make it up;
"It is great," is the word of grown-ups.

It moves on with the train of time,
Composing sweet sounds like a wind-chime.

It includes awesome hues,
Somewhat known as blooming blues.

We waste time in trying to understanding it;
But the actual joy and fun is in living it.

It may include some fights,

PEARL

Yet it is a beautiful present called LIFE.

If it weren't for this poet's

Deadly love of seeking a natural day...

19. One Rainy Day

The pitter-patter, the jibber-jabber,
That I was too heartily fond of:

The world drenched in a sweet blabber,
In a happy harmony embraced,
The rain was a blessing galore,
From those sultry days we faced.

The clouds gurgled at their pleasant whim,
And made us dance aloft;
Toddlers playing in the ground,
Whilst the rain poured soft and sound.

The heart was in a gaily state,
And like the peacocks, searched the sky
To see the dark and bold nimbus clouds fly,
And wished dearly in the heart to soar up high.

Even in the muddy waters, I watched the young lads betray,
Nature's order to stay in, as they then came to play.
The dirty balconies and puddles around, could've been a dismay,
If it weren't for this poet's deadly love of seeking a natural day!

20. A Tree of Birch

There I was a lonely tree,
Having neighbours full of glee:
Roses and daises all galore,
Smiling and dancing evermore.

When I cried, they mocked me,
When I smiled they envied me,
When I danced, they spat on me,
When I talked, they ignored me.

The pansy stared, the lily roared
At me, who to heavens soared.
The Ashoka tree that stood below,
'Scorns' at me, he gladly bestowed.

Huge and many were the Weeping Figs,
Treating me like a rotten pig.
The Lemon Tree, though of manner sour;
Was near in heart but in distance far.

All I bore with a patient shrug,
When one day, she gave me a hug!

I had no hands yet hugged her too,
She lifted me out of the dreadful blue.

A little girl of fifteen, I guess:
Her hair an elegant mess,
Her smile fairer than sunshine,
Her caress just as divine.
My trunk too thin, my leaves all lost,
Gloom welcomed a life of frost;
Beauty left me and so did light,
I was left to the mercy of spite.

My people tore me bit by bit;
But finally a day was sunlit,
When with love of heart bestowed,
My ebbing life began to glow!

She chanted on with her adorable eyes,
Spoke of deceit in love's guise,
Of fickle people living a life of lies,
Yet called hope by saying, 'Time flies.'

That day and every other that came,
I felt could never be the same,
Life got brighter as she visited me daily
And chuckled, danced and sang gaily.

She wrote me imaginary letters,
Enraging the nearby fretters.
Never had love shown in so angelic a form,
Even days so bleak, she kept me warm.

'Bertie the Birch' she named me so,
It lifted me up on days too low;
Reminded me of the friend I had,
For me, too great; for the world, too mad!

Yet, her sweet madness she cherished,
With wonder, our company she relished:
"Our" I say, for she loved my rivals too,
A heart of gold, so pure and true!
Loved me more than them, she said
But, for them, not with atrocity led.

Thus it went on, till she left our mortal world:
Rain became my tears and thunder whirled,
The silenced chuckle tore me apart,
Love spoke no more through her heart.

But the enemies' words made me start,
They had loved her too and were torn apart;
Common grief turned us all kinder of heart,
And to foes of past, empathy it did impart.

In solemn nights she visits me kindly,
And under the eternal moon, we talk fondly;
Through the same tongue we did in ages old
'LOVE', our pure, common language of Gold!

21. A Walk in the Wind

A gleaming heart that was then set,
To pursue the wind;
Through my unkempt hair,
And on my face, I felt gently,
The sweetly blowing air.

In moments as under a tree's shade,
With autumn that precedes summer,
Leaves came pouring out in a mist,
Dried, Yellow, Orange and Red,
Making for me a crunchy bed.
And thus, I passed,
And showered in them;
And as they caressed my face,
They rested on my wind dried lips,
O those leaves, in a heavenly kiss.

The Sun in my mind,
The heart in rain
Of a shower so humbly gained,
I walked through the air;

And to heavens I talked galore,
With wind on my heart's shore,
My face set in a tranquil smile,
With my beloved, in those whiles!

22. The Tale of a Caged Parrot

Its freedom caged,
When its master was engaged.
It fluttered its wings
When they decided to live like kings.

Their cruel ideas and intentions,
Gave the poor parrot many tensions.
Struggling hard to shift its abode,
It never knew it was its master's home.

For his leisure, the master commanded,
"Since very long you were demanded."
Where it dreamt to fly high,
It could not have a relieved sigh.

All its ambitions crushed down,
All its systems shut down;
For it was, just a free bird,
Who never knew the cage would be its world.

23. On a Bright Sunny Day

On a Bright Sunny Day,
In an open field,
I lay on a piece of hay
Under the cerulean curtain of silk;

The gargantuan floating cauliflowers
Or the wisps of milk-like blaze;
There I lay in the blissful shower,
For such was the natural power,
Beyond the words of praise.

The breeze tickling me here and there,
The birds singing now and then,
I stood up staring into the thin air,
I could see no children or men.

My feet were still, stuck to the ground
And I was deliberately spellbound,
For such was the mesmerism of the scene,
It was me and the nature, no one to intervene.

I loved the cicadas' buzzing sound,
And the dragon flies fluttering around;
The golden stalks of well-nourished wheat,
Was actually the farmer's well-won thrift,

They danced with the wind that blew,
Leaving in my eyes a magnificent hue,
That painting of nature deserves a prize,
Which contained flowers and butterflies.

Whenever now I sit to write,
I think there is nothing so might
Except that image that pops up in front of me
Enriching me with heavenly glee.

Under nature's spell I want to grow
To sit and gaze and just adore
And climb through her welcoming door,
I wish to stay there forevermore.
I wish to stay there forevermore.

24. Around The Bonfire

Under the shade of twinkling stars,
The dark black sky was a fear;
The fear faded away with moon's light,
As we all sat around the bonfire.

Enjoying its warmth,
We sang and danced.

On that wonderful night under the dark sky,
We could see the clouds smilingly fly.

Our shivers and fears flew away,
Yet the beauty of the stars never decayed:
The stars all at distant ends,
Ever growing till boundless extents.

The constellations smiling at our earthly forms,
Making us break the usual norms;
For there we stayed for the whole night,
Only to be woken by daylight.

25. Give It For Gaia

Spread the word far and wide,
This is a serious climate fight.

The air is poisoned, the skies pitch-black,
Forests are burning, wildlife we lack.
Temperatures are rising day by day,
With our dagger our mother we slay.

Are we ashamed? Are we aware?
Do, for our mother, we really care?
But you'll ask what is the solution?
To save Earth from this destitution.

Just three words sum it up all,
"Plant a tree" answers the call,
A tree will lay the biggest of foundations,
Spread this message to the farthest nations.

"What good will one tree do?"
Widen your gaze and see it all through.
The life-giver and its sustainer,
All our needs this tree will cater.

Also, don't forget to tell your folks,
Tell them to plant banyans and oaks.
That is indeed the least you can do,
But remember the change starts with you!

Take the charge, make some charts,
Make your art move some hearts,
Your inner voice can shout the loudest,
Bring it out and make Earth, the proudest.

Don't worry; the result would be slow,
But if you persist, stay strong and firm,
The world would go with you, I affirm.
We'll 'restore our earth' soon enough,
We'll make her great and tough.

The forests won't burn, the skies clear,
Now that we wiped our mother's tears:
Joy and bliss is what we'll achieve,
If in the power of planting we believe.
If in the power of planting we believe.

26. Incredible Nature

Incredible Nature,
The best teacher;
It has its own rules,
It can never be befooled.

Its breathtaking mesmerism:
It is the only one with altruism,
Its ways and tactics are amazing,
When I glance at it I remain gaping.

One's greatest friend and companion are trees,
They give you an inspiration without any fees.
The birds chirp and gleefully giggle;
They cut down our tensions as if a sickle.

The roses, carnations, lilies and more;
The coconut trees growing on the sea shore;
The animals, insects are quite a trouble;
It is unarguable that they make us chuckle.

The time spent in its tranquil company
Is a great pleasure for souls better than money.

PEARL

The soothing sights of nature's might
Take away all our frights.

27. Under Sky's Shade

The blue sky,
The white clouds,
The shining sun,
Were all that I saw.

Laying on the green grass,
With a treasure of emotions within me,
I penned down a few words,
The words were a burst out,
I smiled with desire.

The blowing winds mesmerized me,
The pansies and all others bloomed,
My gloominess faded away,
I was happier than ever.

My happiness lied in:
The open place,
The chirping of birds,
The blooming daffodils
And above all, in nature's depths.

"*Smiles do wither,*
But remember flowers wither too;
Doesn't mean new flowers
Can't be born out of the blue."

28. God Is You

God is a belief that people think,
Blindly in this belief you sink.

'Do you believe in god?' I ask,
'Yes, we do', say you at a gasp;
Then I say, 'Who is god?'
'Shiva, Jesus, Allah are gods.'
'But don't you say, "God is one?"'
To protect, your stately "god",
You may pick up a gun.

How can you take its possession?
Often to find god you go on a mission
Why do you think god is superior?
With this feeling you feel yourself to be inferior.

Holy scriptures, priests teach us god,
But have you ever sought for the concept of god?
'Generator, Operator, Destroyer' is it,
Let you and god be together knit:

'I am god' is when you feel,

The power of yourself you seal,
Let you and god be one,
So that in every moment, bliss you earn.

Feel that spirit within you,
Then, the path of godliness you pursue.

29. Success Story

It starts from working hard
Giving it your soul and heart
Avoiding distractions and addictions
You surely need to have some restrictions.

Respecting others, loving them;
Never thinking what will happen in the end.
Believing in yourself and your deeds.
Excellence in your view should be paid heed.

Understanding that we are special:
Can surely win us many medals.
Success is a story to be read till end;
Putting in efforts should be the trend.

Your determination and skills will be tested,
All your talents should be manifested,
Beautify every aspect of excellence,
So that your accomplishments are bold,
Forth and hence.

30. To a New Beginning

I wake up every morning,
Step out of the bed,
Those drudging problems return,
And fill my head.
I say, "Oh, what a dreadful day!'

'Hey mate, listen you haven't lived it all away.
It's just the beginning; you wait and watch,
Don't be in a hurry to push your raft,
Breathe and breathe till you're calmed,
YOU have the control of your magic wand.'

Oh, come on preach it to someone else,
Leave me alone or you'll hear my yells;
I've got meetings, trainings and loads more,
You're the one who has idle time galore.

'Well, I don't say I have no job,
It's just that I can adjust my knob
And stay balanced in every moment,
And keep myself from uttering laments.'

Really? Man, I don't trust you,
How will I deal with all that comes through?
I've worshipped gods all my life,
Yet I don't feel liberation from any strife.

'Then you're the world's biggest clod,
For on the wrong path you've trod.
There is no liberation from any strife,
Or else you may lose living your life.'

Then what is the way?
You tell me today
I am ready to do it in any way,
Let me hear, what you've got to say.

'I will say it loud and slow:
Its real meaning you also know,
"Go on with the flow" is the recipe,
Without any fears of your destiny.
"Be responsible to what the moment brings you,"
And see your life as multi-hued.
All your worries will fade away,
Only YOU shall stay.
For the power this 'YOU' carries within,
Has absolutely no twin.
Just with a smile and head held high,

You walk and walk aware of your sigh.
Let that power unleash,
And see the magic release.'

Well, thanks, it's a lot to digest,
Yet I think I am quite less stressed.
I think you've illumined a spark,
I will try and on that lines embark,
And be the change that sparks within,
All my worries will go in the trash bin.

31. Our Freedom Story

Let's raise our glasses to the warriors of the past,
Who helped us raise our tricolor up the mast!

It started from the revolt of 1857,
When times were as dark as a raven.
When Mangal Pandey gave up the rifle,
The voice of India could not be stifled.

The Indian National Congress was formed,
To reform the British norms.
The partition of Bengal and Surat Split,
Propelled the freedom struggle bit by bit.

The moderates, radicals and the sorts,
Broke all the past records;
The Muslim league took an active part,
And attacked the British as if a dart.

When thousands were slain at Jallianwala Bagh,
Gandhi opted for the Satyagraha marg.
'Simon Go back' was the cry wherever they saw;
Dandi March broke the salt law.

Cripps mission aimed at India's partition,
So congress passed the Quit India Resolution;
74 years ago India's freedom was acknowledged,
The British rule was finally demolished.

Many unsung heroes did die,
So that India could fly,
Above the clouds and the skies,
May my country never agonise.

Today we struggle, strive and toil,
Our doctors burn the midnight oil,
We work together as a team,
In our battle against Covid 19;
We will win for we are together,
These times will surely get better!

32. A World That Never Was

The world I wish for is great of course:

No one with a lie or a curse;

Getting along with one another,

The weather of my dreams is like a feather!

It's soft and gentle

Made of enriched humanity;

People here are pure and humble,

Not possessing the inner chest of vanity.

All of them live in harmony,

Hardly addicted to gain false money,

They are virtuous and good,

Their main motive is to love their neighborhood.

To protect nature is their main concern:

They love it from heaven and earth,

The cows, the birds, all are their friends;

Their virtues towards them have no ends.

The world of my dreams is heavenly
Here no one behaves meanly;
Their unity is worth appreciating,
With their values never depreciating.

33. It is the End

The stars, the earth, life and more,
All are creations of the natural order.

All humans are nature's wondrous creations;
Each with one nose, two eyes, ears and hands,
It gave each one two legs to stand:
All created equal and same in shape,
I wonder why we discriminate.

Nature is creator of sun and moon,
The sun rises in the morn and shines till noon;
The Moon rises at night,
Illumines the dark with its light.

The sun and the moon benefit all,
There is no one short or tall;
Nor is anyone fair or black,
They give heat to one and all.

If they aren't partial in assisting us,
Then why do we say 'me' not us?

I am rich, he is poor;
I am Hindu, he is Sikh;
I worship God, he worships Allah;
And yet we say God is one.

These domestic walls destroy us;
If nature doesn't divide us
Then why do we?
This division should and must end,
Or my dear friend, prejudice is the end.

34. Ferozepur: A Story

75 years of cherishing the freedom glory,
75 years of living the struggle's story,
75 years of changing to rupaiya from pence,
75 years of calling our India Independent.

But who helped attain this eternal joy?
How come this freedom we enjoy?
Was India just as we see it today?
Or was there a heavy price to pay?

I talk of the time around 1857,
When times were as dark as a raven,
I speak of the city on the brink of North-west,
'Ferozepur: Land of Martyrs', we call it best.

This district of Punjab rests on Satluj's bank,
Whose heroes we till today thank,
Whose soil has borne brave warriors of the past,
Who helped raise our tricolor up the mast.

Two events have glorified our history:
Hailing back to the desolate times of misery,

The Battle of Saragarhi recognized worldwide,
Hussaniwala cherishes the Freedom's fight.

12 September 1897, this battle they fought,
Those 21 Sikhs against the Afghans' attacking lot,
Ten thousand attacked the Saragarhi Fort,
The outnumbered match they had to thwart.

Havildar Ishar Singh was their Beacon Light
Who gave the 36th Sikh Regiment their sight.
Sepoy Gurmukh Singh, the steadfast communicator,
Was the regiment's heliograph operator.

Neither the cries of dread or fear,
Nor a single drop of frightful tears,
Glistened on the face of any of these men,
Who strived together as born brethren.

They were lured to give in and bow,
At this thought they furrowed their brow,
Picked up the rifles, and shot some dead,
Their strength was by nationalism fed.

Bhagwan Singh died, Naik Lal was wounded,
Their hatred for Afgans was now deep rooted.
The Afgans blasted the fort's strong walls,
And the Sikhs tried to take cover inside the halls.

The cover failed and all but one were killed,
But the last one was strong-willed,
Gurmukh Singh who had been dormant for too long,
With his battle cry, made the fort's insides throng.

"Bole So Nihal, Sat Sri Akal!" said as he died,
These sons of the soil are India's pride.
The men had died, but the battle was won,
To Afghans, heavy damage had been done.

Today, a Gurudwara stands in my city,
To honour those patriots: bold and witty.
Even the UK celebrates this indelible day,
Of their valour, they speak till today.

Three other names of India's legends,
Can be found engraved on my city's end,
The Indo-Pak division at Hussainiwala Border,
Bears witness to these men's ardour.

Bhagat Singh, Sukhdev, and Rajguru we call them,
They are our inspiring freedom story's gems.
An atheist, a revolutionary, a communist was Bhagat Singh,
To the active and violent struggle he gave wings.

Killed John Saunders with his fellow mates,

The deed was done in December 1928.
Active members of the HSRA,
The trio is honoured till today.

With Batukeshwar Dutt, Delhi's Assembly meet was bombed,
It was fearlessly done on 8 April 1929's morn.
Then, they were arrested and thrown in jail,
But his spirit shouted, "May my country Hail."

They were under trial and to be executed,
Yet they shouted through their voices muted,
"Inquilab Zindabad!" was their eternal cry,
Those sons who held the Tricolour up high!

And they were hanged on 23rd March 1931,
Whole of India's heart they had won.
On Ferozepur's Land these heroes were cremated,
In Satluj's waters their sacred ashes faded.

Today stands a memorial in their honour,
For these martyrs once called bombers,
Who now witness this freedom and love,
From far away, in heaven above.

Recently, we struggled, strived and toiled;
Our doctors burnt the midnight oil,
We worked together as a team,

In our battle against Covid-19.

The virus questioned our freedom and our rights,
And threatened to switch off our life's lights.
But our doctors upheld the eternally burning fire,
Saving thousands from stepping on their pyres.

Against the virus, this battle we did win,
Now again, streets buzz with the usual din.
Life is back to the same old, normal,
With just a garnish of the abnormal.

Well, this time our lesson we did learn,
That upholding freedom goes turn by turn,
The soldiers, doctors, scientists and the citizens galore,
All hold this duty from every door to door.

Blessed with this freedom, these moments we share,
Let's care for our nation in every possible way.
May against the odds, our India never wavers,
Rather just flies high, for today and forever.

35. A Different World

What is this world? Full of delights
With neither worries nor frights.

A painting painted by ourselves
The hues delivered by their inner selves.

A world with no duality
Where people seek to live in reality.

It feels like everything is one,
Could not feel if there is 'anyone'.

Values enrich their hearts and minds,
There is no one of 'separate' kinds.

The spirit of moment lives in them,
Free from belief is their wondrous realm.

Seekers they are called, not atheists;
Their minds are happily confused as if a mist.
They enquire, reason and rationalise,
What is in them they realise.

36. End Competition: End Stress

A race like that of survival of the best,
The competition takes away all our rest.

Comparisons occupy an important place,
You will lose if you reduce your pace.

We pay heed to what others do,
We forget our actions are there too:
Never do we pay regard to our life,
If we lose we begin to cry.

Have we ever thought that competition is atrocious?
It makes good beings, so vicious.

We don't realize two words that help,
So that spirit of 'hard work' we develop.

Move with the moment, working hard
And take away your success card!

Don't plan and prepare,
If you won't, your life will glare.

37. For Triumph

If you know the truth of your life,
You will <u>master your mind, master your life.</u>

The victory lies in the depth of something,
That states <u>the theory of everything.</u>

Be ready to face the difficulty brochures.
Always remember to <u>forge your future.</u>

Don't try to work hard in excess;
Unless you know <u>the seven laws of success.</u>

<u>The power of your subconscious mind</u>
Is the one which will lead you to be refined.

"Poetry is a skill of the soul," they say. But the soul has to be unsheathed from the depths of the earthly form to be skilled. And this unearthing is done by a generous amount of great people.

If gratitude is reminiscent of the beautiful past spent in the wake of some admirable guides, then be it as it may; and let the rest, my courteous heart portray!

38. Dear Mom,

O my dear lovely Mother,
I wish your happiness never withers.

I love you loads,
The one who leads me to success roads.

O the beauty of your abundant heart!
In all my deeds, yours is a big part.

You play the role of my saviour
And lovingly counsel me for my behaviour.

Your love for me is unconditional
That provides me everything additional.

For the times when you read my face
And in your lap I found solace,
I really owe you very much;
You are better than the French and Dutch.

I love you till the moon and beyond!
Of your love, I am forever fond!

39. Dear Dad,

Like the sound of a friendly shore,
All your qualities I adore.
For me all pains you bore;
I heartily admire you ever more.

Ever since I opened my eyes,
You declared I am wise.
I always wish to seek your advice,
Especially when I devise to rise.

Your great virtues are my foundations.
You are the world's most wonderful creation.
Thank you so much for being a guide!
All my talents you amplified.

The world says fathers are strict,
I thought I was tricked,
'Cause you are the gentlest and joyous,
I am sorry if I was disloyal.

I wish always to see a smile on your face.
You corrected me when I fell to disgrace.

PEARL

You have always been so helpful;
For everything you do I will be thankful.

Your unconditional love I will always cherish;
I pray that all your worries perish.
O my happy, beloved inspiration cart,
I love you truly from the core of my heart.

40. Dear Angel,

My love is for you,
My life lies in you.
We fight and play
And share and care,
When we are together we often dare.
I love to call you a cartoon,
To stay with you is a boon.

Words are not enough to describe you,
You are my rainbow's most beautiful hue.
Whatever I show is superficial,
But what lies in my heart is real.

I apologize for all discourtesies and yells,
But now once more I will ring the bells;
Come on!
Let's seal a bond that is never broken
A bond of love and love alone.

Before even telling you, you know everything,
Is it a miracle? I often think,
Maybe that's the reason why we call you ANGEL,

PEARL

You know whether my day is bright or dull.

I never wish to make you cry,
For you I am ready to die.
You understand me, you care for me.
I thank you, but I can't repay thee.

You are a foodie, I know,
A life hacks lover and so,
You are indefinable I say,
Without seeing you,
It's difficult to start the day.

A bond of years we share,
We have had the same food and air.
You always wished for my success,
For me, you are a princess.

I just want to love you ever more,
For you, I always have the open door;
Just a wish that you smile and shine always,
May your life be clear with no haze.

We fight a lot,
But from now we'll not,
For where love lies anger does not,
Let only memories remain of the times we fought.

I love you till space and time,
May I be like a wind-chime:
To add sweet music to your life,
That you may never see the face of strife.

41. Dear Ms. Monika,

As down a hill, a waterfall flows,
Some words for you I compose,
Which flow from deep within my heart,
With feelings as sweet as a treacle tart.

Like a haphazard bee I flew,
Only knowing what I loved to pursue;
You gave me an insight into it,
And the dark sea was finally moon-lit.

I fell in love with your magnanimous words,
My mind flew faster than the birds,
How can someone be so sublimely built?
With knowledge so great, so to the hilt.

Humility runs in your veins;
When you interact, your love rains,
The virtues flow from within you,
All the other things they subdue.

A creature more phenomenal I've never seen,
Who has the proficiency to deal with the unforeseen.

And to this day, gratitude rains,
And I say with pride, not in vain!
For someone so inspirational for me,
For someone who made me, ME!

42. Dear Teachers,

Every day, I woke up in the morn,
With an unloving scorn,
I hated staring at the laptop screen:
"This is not what schooling means!"

And then, reluctantly I'd login for the class
And see a face through that screen of glass.
A loving, bearing, gleeful face ready for the day,
Making my mood from melancholic to gay
And then we'd open our books and start to read,
And in your wake time would flee.

Learning was an amiable delight
With your profound and exquisite sight,
From life-lessons to our academics,
Your expertise defeated the pandemic:
It was an arduous challenge to endure,
With no Corona virus cure;
But you were tough warriors to be defeated,
Your strength is deeply seated
You didn't falter and didn't let us too,
You pulled us out of the blue,

And because of you we did pull through,
After standing in the frightful queue.

I just can't thank you enough
For not letting my future bluff.
I might've passed the school,
But who says there are any rules?
For a child to come visit her parents,
On any day, in any weather.

The results came out and left me amazed,
It was a proof how well I was raised!
By mentors who love, care and share,
You taught me to take risk and dare.

Profound gratitude makes my words too long,
But they do a great too wrong,
For they can't express what my heart feels,
Where lies the depth of bond that seals,
Our relationship in a bubble of respect and admiration,
And reminiscent memories bringing in elation.

The Arcane Aurora

'THE ARCANE AURORA' literally, 'The Mystifying Dawn' is a throwback to a time where in the mysteriousness of my plethoric emotions, there was a rebirth, a revamping of my deeper self. It is to those times I owe this dream come true.

Dawn, the literal word as I hold it, is something, in my estimation, fathomless. The enkindling of the inner infinities, the resounding of dreams, and the unveiling of the cryptic prowess, were all sonic moments which still echo, loud and clear, in my ears. And I never expected that these moments were long in coming. They were spontaneous and eccentric. I never could keep track of the time when I and nature became a mutual family, when words became my refuge, when love presented an unseen aspect of it, when the world appeared in a rhythmic hue…

The shadowy lights spoke to me and I answered them in words so profoundly exquisite that an element self-doubt crept up my heart concerning their composer, me. So astounding were those moments spread happily over space and time that they still leave me spellbound.

Cheers to many more 'Arcane Auroras' which greet me on the way of this existential venture! For this venture never ceases, but is destined from Dawns: where it began, to eternity: where it will end.